Contents

The world's winds

Wind is a valuable source of energy. We can use it to provide the power to work machines, as well as to light and heat our homes, offices and factories.

The term energy comes from the Greek word energos, meaning active or working. Energy sources help other things become active and do work, such as lifting or moving objects. For example, wind power can be used to make electricity. So when you switch on an electric light in your home, the energy to make it work might have come from the power of the world's winds.

What is wind?

Wind is air on the move. We can't see the wind as it blows, but it's easy to see its effects, such as bending trees or the kite flying in the photograph. The movement of air is an important feature of the Earth's climate, and it is caused by heat energy from the Sun. The Sun's heat warms some parts of the world more than others, and this affects the blanket of air that surrounds our planet. Warm air is light and rises, while cool air is heavier and sinks. As the warmer air travels up, cooler air moves in to take its place. It is this movement of air that creates wind.

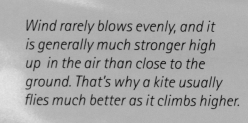

Wind rarely blows evenly, and it is generally much stronger high up in the air than close to the ground. That's why a kite usually flies much better as it climbs higher.

Global pattern

There is an overall pattern to the world's winds. This is caused by the rotation of the Earth, which spins on its axis as it moves around the Sun. The rotation causes winds blowing towards the equator to move generally from east to west. These are often called the trade winds. The winds generally blow the other way further away from the equator. Higher up in the atmosphere, the winds blow mainly from west to east.

RENEWABLE RESOURCE

Wind is a renewable resource, because it can be used again and again and is not in danger of running out. Some other energy sources, such as coal and oil, are burned and used up to produce power. Geothermal, solar, water and biomass power are also renewable forms of energy.

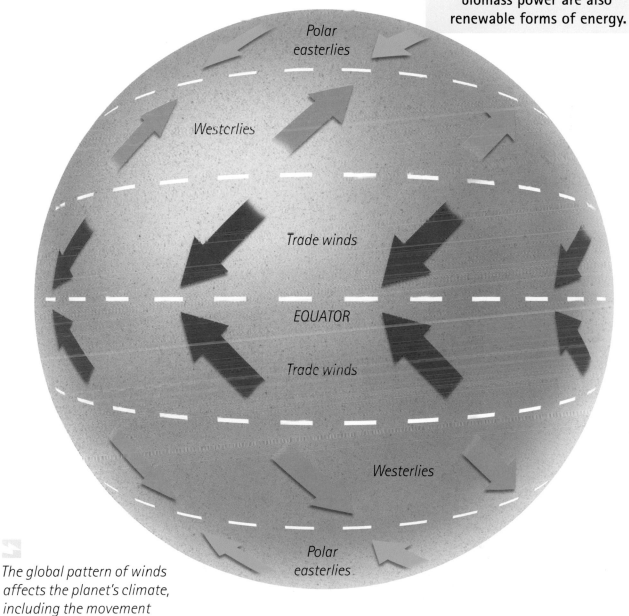

Polar easterlies

Westerlies

Trade winds

EQUATOR

Trade winds

Westerlies

Polar easterlies

The global pattern of winds affects the planet's climate, including the movement of violent storms such as hurricanes.

Sails at sea

The power of the wind has been used to push boats across water for thousands of years.

The ancient Egyptians made their first boats out of bundles of reeds, and by about 3000 BC they had discovered how to use sails that caught the wind. The earliest sailing boats travelled along the River Nile, but sailors soon built larger wooden ships that were strong enough to venture further away from land.

Early trading people used this new method of transport to travel all over the Mediterranean Sea and to other parts of the world, visiting new lands and founding new settlements. The first sails were square-shaped, but later sailors developed triangular sails and other shapes that used the wind better, whichever direction it was blowing from.

These traditional Egyptian sailing boats, called feluccas, are still used on the River Nile today.

Across the oceans

Between AD 800 and 1100, the Vikings of Scandinavia made the best and fastest ships. Danish, Norwegian and Swedish sailors built and sailed their famous Viking longships. When they were near land, the Vikings used oars to row the ships, but on the open sea they were powered by a single square sail. This was made of tough woollen cloth strengthened by strips of leather.

In the 10th century a Norwegian Viking called Erik the Red sailed his longship across the Atlantic Ocean to Greenland. His son Leif Eriksson travelled even further, until he reached a place that he named Vinland (wine land), somewhere on the coast of North America.

Speeding along

Sailing clippers were the fastest wind-powered cargo ships ever built. They did great service in the 19th century, and were called clippers because their speed allowed them to clip days off the normal sailing time of slower ships. This meant they could speed tea from China to Europe, wool from Australia, or people from the east to the west coast of North America during the great California gold rush. Clippers had a light wooden hull and up to six rows of sails on at least three masts, so they had plenty of canvas to catch the wind.

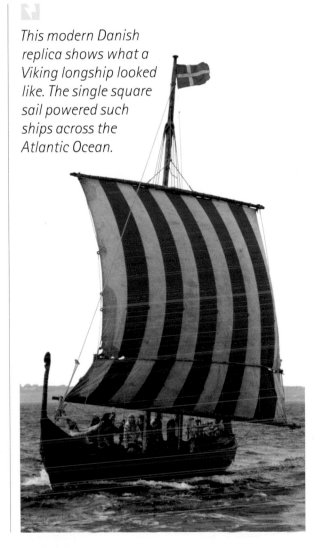

This modern Danish replica shows what a Viking longship looked like. The single square sail powered such ships across the Atlantic Ocean.

Flying Cloud was launched in 1851. This American clipper set a sailing record from New York to San Francisco of just over 89 days.

Windmills

Windmills were among the first machines that humans used instead of their own muscle power. They were probably first built in Persia (modern-day Iran) around the 7th century.

The earliest windmills had sails parallel to the ground that turned on a vertical shaft in a square tower. As the wind moved the sails, the shaft turned a pair of stones to grind grain into flour. By the time of the first European windmills, around 1180, the sails were in the vertical position that we are used to seeing.

Windmills were especially popular in flat regions where there were no fast-flowing rivers or streams to drive waterwheels. These were called post mills, because they were mounted on a wooden post. This meant that the entire mill could turn around to face and catch the wind, depending on the direction from which it was blowing.

This restored English post mill was first built in 1627. The wooden sails are slightly swept back so that the wind hits them at an angle and pushes them sideways. The miller originally fixed cloth to the sails.

Two of the cogwheels inside Pitstone Mill (shown above). Originally made of wood, many cogwheels were later replaced by versions made of iron.

From windshaft to millstone

Most traditional windmills have four sails, which turn in the wind to drive an axle called a windshaft. A toothed cogwheel attached to the windshaft turns another wheel linked to the vertical main shaft. This shaft turns grooved millstones. When grain is poured into holes in the millstones, it is ground into flour. The action of the linked cogwheels means that the millstones turn about five times as fast as the windmill's sails.

Facing the wind

Post mills had a tail pole so that workers could push the whole structure around when the wind changed direction. Later tower mills had a cap for the windshaft and sails, which was also pushed round by hand. Tower mills were made of stronger brick and stone and became landmarks at the edges of towns and villages.

This tower mill, built in 1860, stands at Billingford, in Norfolk. You can clearly see the cap and fantail.

THE FANTAIL

In 1745 an English engineer invented the fantail. This small wheel acts like a rudder on a boat and turns the cap and sails to face the wind. So tower mills with fantails did not have to be pushed round by hand – they used wind power for this process too.

9

Draining and raising water

The Netherlands is famous for its old windmills, but most of them were used to move water rather than to grind grain.

Dutch people have been using wind power to drain the land for centuries. The Netherlands is very flat and low-lying, with almost half the land below sea level, much of which has been reclaimed. The Dutch built banks and dykes around areas to be drained. Windmills then pumped the water into drainage canals that led to rivers and the North Sea. The drained areas are called polders.

The drainage mills used their sails, windshaft and cogs to turn a scoop wheel. This turning wheel scooped up water and poured it into a higher-level ditch. Engineers often built several windmills in a row, so that water could be lifted slightly higher by each one. During the 19th century many windmills were replaced by steam pumps, and some drainage mills were converted to grind grain.

A Dutch tower mill stands at the edge of the polder that it helped create.

Two old windmills on the island of Crete. Some are still powered by the wind, and many are kept working as tourist attractions.

Pumping up water

In southern Europe, where the climate is much warmer and drier, windmills have traditionally been used to pump water up to the surface from beneath the ground. On the Greek island of Crete there were once 10,000 white-sailed windmills. They were originally used to water a large dry plain on the island. Today, most have been replaced by electric and diesel pumps.

American pumps

During the 19th and early 20th centuries, small wind pumps were designed in the United States. These are still used today on some American farms, and they are also popular in dry areas of Australia and South Africa.

These American or western windmills have a windshaft which drives a pump. This sucks up water from a borehole or well sunk into the ground. A vane opposite the wooden or steel wheel turns the windmill to face the wind, like the fantail in tower mills. The water is pumped into a storage tank and used for irrigating the land, as well as for drinking by people and animals.

Inventing wind devices

Today, almost all wind devices are turbines, which are used to generate electricity. The electricity then drives machines in factories or in our homes.

The scientists who developed this technology were building on earlier windmills and drainage pumps, as well as other interesting inventions. Around 2000 years ago, a Greek mathematician called Hero of Alexandria invented the first known wind device – a musical organ. This ancient wind organ had a small wind-driven wheel which drove a piston pump and forced air through organ pipes.

Later, windmills were used for milling and drainage for centuries, until 1592, when a Dutchman named Cornelis Cornelisz built a wind-driven sawmill. This worked by fixing the main shaft to saw blades, which moved up and down and cut lengths of timber as they passed through the mill. It was another 300 years before wind was used to produce electricity.

Windmill dynamo

Charles Francis Brush (1849–1929) was an American inventor who devised a street-lighting system in Cleveland, Ohio, in 1878. Ten years later, he built a giant windmill with an iron tower and a 17-metre wide wheel made up of 144 wooden blades. It also had an enormous tail that turned the wheel into the wind.

This was probably the world's first electricity-generating windmill. The slowly turning wheel drove a dynamo, or simple generator, which was connected to more than 400 batteries in the basement of Brush's house.

MEASURING THE WIND

An anemometer is a device that measures wind speed. The first working wind-meter was a spinning disk invented in Italy in 1450. Exactly 400 years later, an Irishman named Thomas Robinson invented the version still used today, in which cups catch the wind.

Brush's windmill dynamo, which the inventor used to light his house and to run electric motors.

Wind electrician

In 1890 Poul La Cour (1846–1908), a Danish high-school teacher and inventor, began using windmills to generate electricity. His windmills had a more traditional European design, with four or six sails mounted on wooden or iron towers. They were attached to turbine buildings in the Danish village of Askov. In 1903 La Cour founded the Society of Wind Electricians, and he published the world's first journal on the subject of wind electricity. His pioneering work meant that wind power was used to produce electricity all over Denmark in the early 20th century. Later in the century, this interest dropped, but today Denmark is the world's fourth largest producer of wind energy.

Modern wind turbines

Most modern wind turbines (or aerogenerators) look like up-to-date versions of traditional windmills.

They generally have three long, narrow rotor blades, though some versions have two blades or even a single blade. The rotor faces the wind and turns a shaft that is parallel to the ground. Because of this, they are known as horizontal axis wind turbines (or HAWTs for short). The reason they don't have more blades, like American wind pumps, is that they have to withstand very strong forces in high winds.

Huge cranes lift rotor blades to the top of a turbine tower. Helicopters are sometimes used for this job.

The design of these vertical-axis turbines beside the Welsh coast is known as cross-arm or sailwing. These turbines look quite different from traditional windmills.

Vertical axis

In vertical axis wind turbines (or VAWTs), the windshaft or main axle stands upright. The blades do not need to be swivelled around to face the wind, as they are spun by winds from any direction. In the vertical design the generator can be close to the ground, which is another advantage because it makes it easier to get at. But generally experts have found that VAWTs are not as efficient as horizontal turbines, so very few have been built. Nevertheless, engineers go on looking for new designs that may be more efficient in future.

Darrieus design

In the 1920s a French engineer named Georges Darrieus invented a new design for the wind turbine. This looked like a giant eggbeater, with up to four curved blades attached to a vertical shaft. Darrieus turbines are still used today.

The blades have an aerofoil shape, like the wings of an aeroplane, which creates a force called lift and pushes the blades round very fast. The disadvantage of this design is that the blades do not easily start to spin from a standing start, so electricity has to be used to kick-start them.

A row of Darrieus 'eggbeater' turbines.
Each one is held firm by steel cables.

Generating electricity

A wind turbine uses a generator to produce electricity, using a system that was invented in the 19th century.

In 1831 the British scientist Michael Faraday discovered that he could create electricity by moving a magnet through a coil of copper wire. This led to the invention of the electric generator, which works by changing mechanical energy into electrical energy. In the case of a wind turbine, the power of moving air provides the mechanical energy by turning rotor blades.

The blades are connected to a shaft, which is also attached to a generator. Inside the generator, the shaft makes magnets spin inside wire coils to produce electricity, which is carried away by a cable. The turbine's cable joins up to a main electricity network at the nearest available point.

Inside a wind turbine. The pod acts as weatherproof protection for all the mechanical and electrical parts.

gearbox

generator

rotor blade

Inside the pod

The generator and other pieces of equipment are housed inside a streamlined nacelle, or pod. This turns according to the direction of the wind. Sensors in a small wind vane send signals to a computer, which works out the best direction and operates an electric motor. Inside the pod, the turning shaft is linked to a set of gears, which increase its speed so that it can turn the generator more effectively.

Speed limits

Very strong winds could spin a wind turbine's blades too fast and make it dangerous. To prevent this, electronic control systems alter the angle of the rotor blades as well as the direction they face. This tilting of the blades is called pitch control, and it affects their speed by twisting them so that they do not catch the wind so well.

Many turbines also have automatic braking systems inside the pod, which slow the speed of the shaft if it is turning too fast. All these systems are checked regularly by engineers.

WITHSTANDING WIND POWER

Turbine manufacturers have to allow for extreme wind conditions when designing and building modern turbines. They need to make sure that the blades will not be torn off and that turbine towers will not be blown down. This is vital, because the world's largest wind turbines are as high as 100 metres tall.

Two service engineers check a wind turbine's systems. This photograph shows how large the pod is.

Wind farms

A large wind turbine may produce about one megawatt (or one million watts) of power. A large coal-fired power station produces up to 5000 megawatts.

In the late 20th century, engineers realized that they could group wind turbines together to make power plants. These groups are called wind farms (or sometimes wind parks), and the cables from their turbines join together to feed a main power line.

   The farms are built where there are generally strong, steady winds all year round. Exposed coasts, mountain passes and hilltops are good locations. The turbines are not placed too close together, because their rotors need the full force of the wind. Very often a wind farm is designed in rows of turbines.

A small wind farm on one of the islands of Hawaii.

California wind rush

In the early 1980s wind farms started to spring up in different parts of the world. The largest was in California, where planners decided that wind power could be important in the future. Some newspapers called this a wind rush (like the California gold rush 130 years earlier).

At Altamont Pass, a wind farm of 6000 turbines was built, which today produces more than a quarter of all the wind power generated in California. The location works well because air rising from a hot valley to the east sucks cooler air from the Pacific Ocean into the pass through the hills.

Offshore opportunities

Offshore waters often provide the best wind conditions for turbines. Wind farms have already been set up off the coast of Britain, Denmark and other European countries. They are generally built in shallow waters, so the towers or pylons can be firmly attached to the seabed. The Horns Rev wind farm, off the west coast of Denmark, was built in 2002. It is made up of 80 turbines, each 70 metres tall, which cover an area of 20 square kilometres in the North Sea.

Wind turbines at Altamont Pass, California. Many of the turbines are designed to face downwind (away from the wind) rather than into it.

At the Horns Rev wind farm, the turbines are set more than 500 metres apart. They stand in shallow water 14 kilometres off the Danish coast.

ONSHORE VERSUS OFFSHORE

Many people who dislike the look of wind farms on land think that more should be developed offshore. But planners have to make sure that offshore turbines do not cause danger to shipping.

Small schemes

Wind power can also be produced on a small scale, and aerogenerators have become a popular way for individuals or small communities to produce their own electricity.

Companies sell modern turbines that produce 1 kilowatt of electricity – one thousandth as much as large, commercial versions. In many countries they can be connected to the national grid, so that any extra electricity is sold and used by others, while mains is available if needed.

Ecovillages

Ecovillages are communities of people who try to live in a way that protects and preserves the natural environment as much as possible. The villagers do all they can to keep their soil, water and air clean, and they prefer to use renewable energy. Many ecovillages rely on wind and solar power for their electricity, because the villagers consider these environmentally friendly methods. Their experiences provide interesting research for others.

A small wind turbine produces electricity for a community in northern China.

ENERGY WHERE IT IS NEEDED

One of the great advantages of
small schemes is that electricity can
be produced very close to where it
is used. This means there is no need
for expensive pylons and heavy
transmission lines, so the systems have
very little effect on the environment.

Farming the wind

Individual small-scale wind turbines can be very useful
for farming communities. They have been used for many
years for pumping water (see page 10), and now they
are increasingly used for electricity production.

There are several schemes in Britain and elsewhere,
where farmers have found their own small wind turbine so
successful that at times they produce more electricity than
they need. They sell the extra power by supplying it to the
national grid, the network of power lines that supplies
mains electricity to most homes. This is a good use of
natural resources.

*At Etosha National Park in
Namibia, some waterholes
have wind pumps to bring
water to the surface. These
are especially helpful in
times of drought.*

Around the world

Wind blows all over the world, on all continents and across all oceans, which means it could be used everywhere as an energy source.

Wind turbines already operate in the warm tropics and the cold polar regions, including those being developed to power scientific bases in Antarctica. At the beginning of the 21st century, two thirds of the world's wind power is produced in Europe. Germany produces most, followed by Spain and Denmark. The Danes use wind to produce about 12 per cent of their electricity.

The other big producers in the world are the United States and India. But this energy source is becoming more important in other areas too, especially in developing countries where many communities are not provided with electricity by a national grid.

Chinese developments

China has used windmills for centuries to grind grain and pump water to irrigate the land. Today, coal-fired power stations and hydroelectric dams produce most of China's electricity, but interest in wind potential is growing. Strong winds blow from the desert areas in

These technicians are working on wind-turbine parts at a large factory in northern Germany. Both Germany and Denmark export turbines and wind technology, as well as using them at home.

the north-west of the country over the steppes of Mongolia and down to the south-east coast and the Pacific Ocean. In 2003 a German company built a wind farm near the coast. This technology may develop further in China, which is the world's second-highest user of electricity (after the US).

Windswept Patagonia

The Patagonian region of South America is an important source of energy for Argentina. Here rivers are dammed to produce electricity, and there are oil fields and coal mines. Since the beginning of the 21st century, wind has been an additional energy source. This is not surprising, since Patagonia is a windswept plateau famous for its dry, blustery climate. The villages near the wind farms that are springing up now benefit from wind-powered electricity.

The strong winds on the plains of Patagonia have shaped the branches of this pine tree.

Renewable benefits

As a renewable energy source, wind has many benefits compared with non-renewable sources such as fossil fuels.

Winds will continue to blow so long as the Sun warms the Earth, but our planet's fossil fuels are gradually running out. Experts predict that the world's reserves of coal will last little longer than 200 years, while reserves of oil and gas may run out in about 60 years' time. Yet most electricity today is produced by power stations burning fossil fuels.

So it makes sense for governments to try to increase their use of renewable resources such as wind and water. Wind power is also considered to be 'clean and green', because producing it does not harm the environment. For all these reasons, wind is a popular source of energy with most people, who would like more power generated by wind.

An oil refinery gives off harmful gases. Renewable energy sources are much less damaging to the environment.

Helping the environment

When fossil fuels are burned, they release a gas called carbon dioxide. Producing too much of this and other gases makes the Earth's atmosphere trap more of the Sun's heat, creating a 'greenhouse effect'. Experts believe that this has led to the world gradually heating up, and that this global warming might lead to a rise in sea levels as polar ice melts. Using renewable sources such as wind helps reduce these problems.

NEED FOR POWER

Small turbines need a wind speed greater than 15 kilometres per hour, which is called a gentle breeze by weather-forecasters. Large towers usually need a wind speed of 20 kph (called a moderate wind). There is usually more wind during the day than at night and that is when people use more electricity.

Safe and reliable

Wind energy is safe. If turbines are sensibly placed and regularly serviced, there is very little risk of them causing any harm. They automatically shut down in high winds. Although winds in any particular place are variable, turbines can generally produce electricity about three-quarters of the time.

Wind farms work perfectly well with cattle farms.

Wind power is versatile, and small turbines can be put to many different uses. This one powers an electric fence, which keeps animals from straying without harming them.

Potential problems

All forms of energy production have some impact on the environment. In the case of wind power, the effects are generally local, which makes them easier to put right if necessary.

The fast-moving blades of turbines can affect radar equipment, so it would not be sensible to build a wind farm near an airport. Another potential problem is cost, as many people believe that wind-produced electricity is bound to be expensive.

In fact, the cost of generating electricity from wind has fallen dramatically in recent years, as wind farms have become more efficient. At the same time, other sources of energy (especially oil) have become much more expensive. Nevertheless, some people are concerned about wind power's effects on wildlife and the look of the countryside.

ENDANGERING BIRDS AND BATS

Many people are concerned that wind farms kill birds and bats that fly into their towers and blades. This appears to be a problem if turbines are placed on a flying path that is regularly used by migrating birds. Environmentalists say this is the case with Altamont Pass in California (see page 19), which is a known route for many eagles, hawks and owls. The solution is to locate wind farms away from the known routes and territories of birds and bats, especially those of endangered species.

Sight and sound

Large wind turbines can spoil the look of a landscape, and many people living in the country do not want to see them from their windows. Nevertheless, the slim towers are less ugly than other power plants, and they are not polluting.

If you go close to them, older turbines can be a bit noisy, with swishing blades and mechanical clunks. Manufacturers claim that improved technology has made modern turbines much quieter. Turbines facing downwind make more noise than those turned into the wind.

Hilltops make an effective location for turbines, but they may be visible for miles around.

Flocks of migrating birds could be most in danger from wind farms.

Future trends

Wind and other renewable energy sources will become more and more important in future, as the world's demand for energy and electricity goes on increasing.

Demand for electricity is forecast to nearly double over the next 25 years. Wind power is the fastest-growing energy sector, but it still generates just a small percentage of the total energy we use and it will never be able to meet huge increases in demand.

To help customers who want to avoid damaging the environment as much as possible, electricity companies in some countries offer what they call 'good energy', meaning energy from renewable sources. There will probably be more schemes like this in future, and people will also be encouraged to use energy more wisely and sparingly. At the same time, engineers and inventors will continue to search for new ways to harness the power of the wind.

A demonstration in Japan against power stations' emissions of carbon dioxide (CO_2). Renewable energy sources will help in future.

New ideas

Many coastal countries believe that the future lies in offshore wind farms. Engineers are looking at new ways of making this possible, including putting wind turbines on floating rafts. Others think that we could make better use of the stronger winds that blow high up in the sky.

Scientists in the Netherlands are working on a system called a laddermill, which consists of a loop

of kites that rotate in the wind and turn a cable. Another system, called a gyromill, is being developed by an Australian professor. This would fly up to 4500 metres above the Earth, sending back electricity generated by spinning rotors.

A prototype gyromill. Will devices like this produce electricity in the future?

Futuristic buildings

In future it may be possible to include wind turbines in tall buildings, and this is already being planned. Some architects and designers are working on a vertical set of turbines built into a skyscraper. Others think it would be easier to include fewer turbines near the top of a tall building. Engineers have not yet solved all the practical problems, but a successful design could allow a giant skyscraper to generate its own electricity.

An artist's impression of a twin-tower skyscraper with its own source of power.

# Glossary

aerogenerator A wind turbine that generates electricity.

anemometer A device that measures wind speed.

atmosphere The blanket of air that surrounds the Earth.

axis An imaginary straight line around which something spins.

climate Weather in a region over a long period of time.

clipper A fast sailing ship with tall masts and many sails.

cogwheel A toothed wheel that fits together with another wheel to turn it.

dyke A wall or bank of earth or stone built to hold back water and stop flooding.

dynamo A machine that turns mechanical energy into electrical energy.

environmentalist A person who is concerned about and acts to protect the natural environment.

equator An imaginary line around the middle of the Earth.

fantail A small wheel on a windmill that keeps the main sails facing the wind.

fossil fuel A fuel (such as coal, oil and natural gas) that comes from the remains of prehistoric plants and animals.

generator A machine that turns mechanical energy into electrical energy.

greenhouse effect The warming of the Earth's surface (called global warming) caused especially by pollution from burning fossil fuels.

hull The main body of a ship.

irrigate To water (land) in order to help crops to grow.

megawatt One million watts (a watt is a unit of power).

millstone A large round stone used to grind grain.

nacelle A streamlined housing, or pod.

pitch control Changing the angle of blades to control the speed at which they spin.

plateau A flat area of high land.

power station A plant where electricity is generated.

pylon A tall metal tower that supports power cables.

rotor The spinning assembly and blades of a wind turbine.

sawmill A mill in which wood is sawn into planks.

tropics The warmest part of the world near the equator.

turbine A machine with rotating blades.

windshaft The shaft or pole to which the sails of a windmill are attached.

Index